"We're in science fiction now, aren't we?" said Jason on the first day. "We are in Shine" said Pattie firmly, "And no monsters will come."

Starting a fresh life on an unexplored planet is the challenge facing Pattie, her sister and the rest of the group from Earth. They may only take basic tools and one book each. At first Shine seems a friendly place. The group build their houses, tell stories and discover the inflammable jellyfish. But the planet holds fear as well — of the terrifying-looking Moth people and the even greater fear of the loss of their harvest.

When the wheat starts coming up hard and glassy, and it looks as if no food will grow, Pattie and her brother and sister are ready to take a desperate gamble to try and make survival on Shine possible.

Shine was previously published in hardback as *The Green Book.*

SHINE

SHINE

by

Jill Paton Walsh

Macdonald

Illustrations by Sue Smith

A Macdonald Book

First published in Great Britain in 1981 as *The Green Book*

This edition published in 1988 by
Macdonald & Co (Publishers) Ltd
London and Sydney

All characters in this publication are fictitious, and any resemblance to real persons, living or dead, is purely coincidental.

British Library Cataloguing in Publication Data
Paton Walsh, Jill
Shine. I. Title
823'.914[J] PZ7

ISBN 0-356-13462-8
ISBN 0-356-13463-6 Pbk

Printed and bound in Great Britain by
Robert Hartnoll (1985) Ltd, Cornwall

Macdonald & Co (Publishers) Ltd
Greater London House
Hampstead Road
London NW1 7QX

A BPCC plc company

Contents

For Robert and Matthew
and Kate

Chapter One

Father said, "We can take very little with us." The list was in his hand. "Spade, saw, file, axe, for each family. Seeds, etc., will be provided. Iron rations will be provided. For each voyager a change of clothing, a pair of boots, *one* or *two* personal items *only*; e.g., a favourite cooking pan, a musical instrument (small and light), a picture (unframed). Nothing under this heading will be taken if it is bulky or heavy, fragile or perishable. One book per voyager."

It was easy to pack. We were allowed so little, and we didn't have to bother about leaving anything tidy behind us. Only the books caused a little delay. Father said, "I must take this." He showed us an ugly big volume called *A Dictionary of Intermediate Technology*. "But you must choose for yourselves," he said. "It wouldn't be fair of me to choose for you. Think carefully."

We didn't think. We were excited, disturbed, and we hadn't really understood that everything else would be left behind. Father looked wistfully at the shelves. He picked up *The Oxford Complete Shakespeare*.

"Have you all chosen your books?" he asked. "Yes," we told him. He put the Shakespeare back.

We had time to waste at the end. We ate everything we could find.

"I don't want to eat iron," Pattie said, but nobody knew what she meant.

Then Father got out the slide projector, and showed us pictures of holidays we had once had. We didn't think much of them.

"Have they all gone brownish with age, Dad?" said Joe, our brother, the eldest of us.

"No," said Father. "The pictures are all right. It's the light that has changed. It's been getting colder and bluer now for years ... but when I was young it was this lovely golden colour, just like this — look."

But what he showed us — a beach, with a blue sea, and the mother we couldn't remember lying on a towel, reading a book — looked a funny hue, as though someone had brushed it over with a layer of treacle.

Pattie was glad that Father wasn't going to be able to take the slide projector. It made him sad.

And the next day we all went away, Father and Joe, and Sarah, and Pattie, and lots of other families, and left the Earth far behind.

When this happened, we were all quite young, and Pattie was so young that later she couldn't remember being on the Earth at all, except those few last hours, and even the journey was mostly forgotten. She could remember the beginning of the journey, because it was so exciting. When we could undo our seat belts, and look out of the windows, the world looked like a Chinese paper lantern, with painted lands upon it, and all the people on the ship looked at it, and some of the grown-ups cried. Father didn't cry; he didn't look, either.

Joe went and talked to Father by and by, but Sarah

and Pattie stood at a porthole all day long, and saw the world shrink and shrink and diminish down till it looked like a round cloudy glass marble that you could have rolled on the palm of your hand. Pattie was looking forward to going past the moon, but that was no fun at all, for the ship passed by the dark side, and we saw nothing of it. And then we were flying in a wide black starry sky, where none of the stars had names.

At first there were voices from the world below, but not for long. The Disaster from which we were escaping happened much sooner than they had thought it would, and after two days the ship was flying in radio silence, alone, and navigating with a calculator program on the computer, and a map of magnetic fields.

The journey was very boring. It was so long. The spaceship was big enough to frighten us when we thought of it flying through the void. Joe kept telling Pattie not to worry.

"Heavy things *don't* fall down in space," he told her. "There's nowhere for them to fall; no gravity."

"When I knock things over, they fall down, just like at home," Pattie said, doubtfully.

"That's just the ship's gravity machine, making it happen inside the ship," said Joe. "To make us feel normal."

But the ship was *small* enough to frighten us too, when we thought of spending years inside it.

"We will still be here when I'm fourteen!" said Joe, as though he found that as hard to believe as Pattie found the lack of gravity.

"Better get used to it," said Sarah. We had pills to make us sleep a lot of the time, but the rules said everyone had to be awake some of each forty-eight hours. When people were awake, they played games — Monopoly, and Go, and backgammon, and chess, and Mastermind, and Space Invaders, which were all on the ship's computer and could be played with the video screens. And one of the grown-ups had even brought along as his special luxury a funny hand set for playing chess which let you play it with another person instead of with the computer. When we weren't playing games, we could read the books we had brought. Joe asked Father why there were no books to read on the computer screens.

Father told us that all the new, well-equipped spaceships belonged to big wealthy countries. They had flown off to find distant, promising-looking planets.

"We were the bottom of the barrel," he said, "the last few to go from an old and poorer country, and only an old ship available, and no time to outfit it properly. Our computer was intended for exploration journeys, not for colonization. It has no space memory; it can barely manage our minimum needs. And there was so little fuel we couldn't get lift-off with anything extra on board — no useful livestock, like sheep or cows; just ourselves, and what the organizers thought we needed for survival. But we are lucky to be away at all, remember, and they allocated us a much nearer destination so that our old ship could get us somewhere."

There were some chickens in cages on the ship, with two very noisy cocks who had lost their sense of timing in the flight through darkness and crowed at all the wrong times when we were trying to sleep. And there were rabbits too; we could let them out and play with them. Rabbits are fun when you are very small and like furry things, but they aren't much fun, really. You can't teach them tricks. All they ever think about is munching. And when we got bored with rabbits, all we had was that one book each to go back to. Of course, we tried to read slowly. "Read each sentence at least twice, before you read another," the rule books said, under "Helpful Suggestions." But Sarah couldn't read that slowly. At home she read four or five books every week. She finished her book quickly and then wanted to borrow Pattie's

Pattie wouldn't let her. So she swapped with Joe, and read his. He had brought *Robinson Crusoe.* Sarah didn't much like *Robinson Crusoe.*

"You'd better think about him, old girl," Joe said to her. "That island is just like where we're going, and we have to scratch a living on it, just like Crusoe."

"Well, I hope we don't have to pray and carry on like him," said Sarah.

Joe didn't like Sarah's book any better than she liked his. Hers was called *The Pony Club Rides Again.* Joe didn't like horses, and he couldn't resist telling Sarah that, after all, she would never see a horse again as long as she lived.

So then they both wanted to borrow Pattie's book. Pattie wouldn't lend it.

"I haven't finished it myself yet," she kept saying. "It's not fair. You finished yours before you had to lend it."

In the end, Father made her give it to them. It was thin and neat, with dark green silky boards covered with gold tooling. The edges of the pages were gilded and shiny. It had a creamy silk ribbon to mark the place, and pretty brown and white flowered end-papers. And it was quite empty.

'There's nothing in it!" cried Sarah, staring.

"It's a commonplace book," said Joe.

"What's that?" asked Sarah.

"A sort of jotter, notebook thing, for thoughts you want to keep."

"And she's been pretending to read it for months!" said Sarah, beginning to giggle. They both laughed and laughed. Other people came by and asked what the joke was. Everyone laughed.

"Oh, Pattie, dear child," said Father when he heard about it. He didn't laugh, he looked a mixture between sad and cross.

"It was my choose," said Pattie very fiercely, taking

her book back and holding it tight.

Father said, "She was too young. I should have chosen for her. But no use crying over spilt milk."

We did get used to being on the ship, in the end. A funny thing happened to the way people felt about it. At first, everyone had hated it, grumbled all the time about tiny cubicles, about no exercise, about nothing to do. They had quarrelled a lot. Grown-up quarrelling isn't very nice. We were luckier than most families; we didn't seem to quarrel, though we got very cross and scratchy about things, just like other people. But time went by, and people settled down to playing games, and sleeping, and talking a little, and got used to it, and so when at last everyone had had four birthdays on the ship, and the journey had been going on for what seemed like forever and ever, and the Guide told us all there were only months to go now, people were worried instead of glad.

"We shall be lucky if we can walk more than three steps, we're so flabby," said Father, and people began to do pushups in their cabins, and line up for a turn on the cycle machine for exercising legs.

Joe began to ask a lot of questions. He didn't like the answers he got and he talked to Pattie and Sarah about it after lights-out in sleeping times.

"They just don't know what this place is going to be like," he told them. "They *think* it should support life; they know there is plant growth on it, and they suppose that means we could grow wheat. But there may be wild animals, or any kind of monster people on it already, they don't know."

"Couldn't there possibly be wild ponies, Joe?" said Sarah.

"No, sis, I don't think so," said Joe, very kindly. "And if this place isn't any good, we can't go anywhere else. The fuel won't last. All they've got for us if it isn't any good are pills."

"I don't want to take pills," said Pattie.

"We'll have to, if all the others are taking them," Sarah told her. "We couldn't be left alone."

"I think we ought to be allowed to choose," said Pattie.

"Oh, Pattie!" said Joe, grinning at her from his bunk. "You're a fine one to talk about choosing! What good is your choosing, you goose!"

Chapter Two

A time came when we reached the light of a new sun. Bright golden light filled the spaceship from the starboard portholes. The cocks woke up and crowed as if for all the missing mornings on the whole long trip. The sun warmed the ship, and made it hard to sleep at sleeping time. And then the new planet loomed up on the starboard side. It looked unlike the Earth, said the grown-ups, who could remember what the Earth had looked like. It was redder and shinier; it had no cloud drifts around it. When it got near, it looked like maps in bright colours. It didn't look green. People spent all day looking anxiously through the portholes at it, trying to guess the meaning of what they could see. Just before touchdown, we could all see a land with mountains, craggy and rocky, and large lakes lying on the land surface everywhere; but as the ship came in to land, nightfall was racing us across the ground — a big black shadow, engulfing everything, moving faster than we were ourselves, its crescent edge going at a dizzy speed, and leaving us behind, so that we landed in total darkness. It was an auto-control landing anyway. It happened smoothly. The ship landed at a steep angle, but immediately straightened up by levelling its podlike legs. Then it switched off its own gravity and hummed quietly into run-down cycles.

When the gravity machine switched off, everyone felt lightheaded, and, indeed, light. The planet's own gravity was less than the ship had got us used to. Pattie found she could jump up and touch her cabin roof, and land without thudding enough to make anyone cross. Everyone felt full of energy, and eagerness to get out. But the Guide said the ship must be kept locked till daylight. So little was known, it would be dangerous to go out.

Arthur, the head of one of the families, said he would go and have a look, at his own risk, and then the Guide spoke to us very sternly.

"It's natural to feel excited," he said. "But this is not a holiday. We are a handpicked group; we are the minimum number that can possibly survive and multiply. Between us we have the skills we require. But the loss of a single member of our party will endanger the survival of us all. There is no such thing, Arthur, as 'your own risk.' Not any more. And may we all remember that."

We sat around, fidgeting, restless, talking together in lowered voices, waiting for dawn. None of the games interested us now. Pattie couldn't sleep, though Father made her lie down on her bunk. The feeling of suspense, the unfamiliar rhythm of the machines running themselves toward shutdown, the altered pitch of the voices around her kept her awake so late, so long, that when dawn broke at last she was fast asleep and did not see it.

But Sarah told her it had come like a dark curtain being swept aside in a single rapid movement; for a few minutes there was a deep indigo light, and after that, brilliance.

The Guide walked around the ship, looking out of each porthole in turn. All that he could see was rocks, white and grey, rather glittery crags, all very near the ship, blocking any distant view. They gave Arthur a breathing mask and put him through the inner door to the ship's main hatch, closing it behind him before he opened the outer door. He came back very quickly. "Come out," he said "The air is good."

So we trooped down the ramp and found ourselves in the shadow of the ship, in a narrow gully between one rock face and another. It seemed to be a sort of hanging valley in a hill. A tiny runnel of flowing clear liquid threaded between rocks in the bottom of the dip, over a bed of silver-white sand and pebbles. Malcolm, the party's chemist, took a sample of the stream in a little specimen bottle, to test it.

Pattie was so sleepy after the night before that she could hardly walk, and Father picked her up and carried her, nodding with drowsiness, rather than leave her alone in the ship. She went in his arms, up the slope towards a gentle saddle between one side of the valley and the other, where all the others were walking. It was easy to walk, even up the slope; Pattie felt light and easy to carry. So up we all went to the rim of the hollow, and looked over.

Before us lay a wide and gentle plain sloping to the shores of a round wide lake some miles across. Beyond the lake, a very high mountain with perfectly symmetrical slopes rose into the sky, topped with snow. A mirror image of the lovely mountain hung inverted in the lake, quite still, for the surface was like glass, perfectly unruffled by even the slightest impulse of the air. The surface of the plain was grey and silver, shining like marcasite in places, in others with a pewter sheen. To the left and right of the plain, on gentle hills, were wide sweeps of woodland, with quite recognizable and normal trees, except that the leaves upon them were not green but shades of red, and shining, like the blaze of an amazing autumn. It was very beautiful, and perfectly silent, and perfectly still.

The children ran forward onto the open expanse of land before them, shouting. And at once we were limping, crying, and hopping back. We were still wearing the soft ship slippers we had been given to keep down the noise in the corridors of the spacecraft, and the pretty grey grass and flowers had cut through the thin leather at once, and cut our feet. The Guide ordered the crate of boots to be brought from the store and unpacked. Someone fetched ointment and sticking plaster. Meanwhile, we stooped and picked the sharp plants, which broke easily in our fingers when gathered; they seemed to be made of glass, sharp and shining like jewels. But as soon as we all had boots on, we could walk over them safely, for the growth was crushed beneath the soles, as fragile and as crunchy to walk on as the frost-stiffened grass of winter on Earth.

We all walked over the crisp and sparkling frost plain, down toward the shores of the lake. It took an hour to reach it. The lake shore was a wide silver beach, made of soft bright sand, like grains of worndown glass. And all the time we walked toward the lake, it did not move, or ruffle, even enough to shake the curtains of reflected mountain and reflected sky that hung in it. And though the air smelled good and sweet to breathe, it was windless, and as still as the air in a deep cave underground. Only the little rivulet that followed us across to the lake from the crag valley where the ship had lodged moved; it chuckled gently from stone to stone, and sparkled as brightly as the glass leaves and grass. When we got to the beach, Pattie went to look where it joined the lake, to see if it would make some splash or ripples for just a little way, but it seemed to slide beneath the surface at once and made only the faintest ripple ring, quickly dying in the brilliant mirror of the lake.

"I think we may be lucky," said the Guide. "I think this place is good."

People laughed, and some of the grown-ups kissed each other. The children ran to the edge of the lake and made it splash. Jason's mother ran along the beach, calling to the paddling children not to drink from the lake until Malcolm had made sure it was water. Everyone was thirsty from walking, and the lake looked clear and good, but we all obediently drank from the flagons of recycled water from the ship.

"Right," said the Guide. "We shall begin the settlement programme. And first we need to name the place we are about to build. The instructions suggest that the youngest person present should give the name. That can't include the real babies, obviously; Pattie or Jason — which is the youngest?"

Jason's mother and Pattie's father spoke together.

"It is Pattie, by a few days," said Father. "Well, Pattie, where are we?"

"We are at Shine, on the first day," said Pattie, solemnly.

"Good girl," said the Guide. "This place, then, is Shine. And now we must all work, and fast, for we do not know how long the days are here, or what dangers there may be." And he began to hand out jobs to each one in turn.

So people went back to the ship to unload the land truck, fill it with tents and food and sleeping bags, and bring them to the shore. Malcolm went to complete his tests for water. A work party was formed to unload the land hopper and put it together. The land hopper would glide or fly just above the ground, and let us explore quickly, and then it would run out of fuel and be of no more use. And the Guide had two men standing with guns ready, one each side of the camping ground, in case of wild beasts, or enemies.

"In science fiction, bullets go right through things and they come right on anyway, roaring, urrrrrr!" said Jason. "And we're in science fiction now, aren't we, so what good are guns?"

"We are in Shine," said Pattie. "And no monsters will

come." Jason hadn't talked to her much on the flight; he was much shorter than she, and he thought she was older. But now he had found that, although she was taller, she was younger, and he got friendlier.

There was no job for either, so they watched Joe setting up a tally stick. It was a huge plastic post with rows and rows of holes in it, and black pegs to move in the holes.

"What's it for, Joe?" they asked.

"It's a calendar," said Joe. "We have to count the days here, or we'll lose track. All the things on the ship will run down and stop working — clocks, calculators, everything. So this thing just keeps a count — you move one hole for each day. You move the peg, and you remember when you are."

"A tree of days," said Pattie.

The grown-ups brought a stove from the ship, and a can of fuel, and set it up to cook supper on the beach, for the sand was soft and easy to sit and walk on, unlike the grey glass grass. A ring of tents went up around the stove. Malcolm decided that the little stream and the huge lake were both good water, fit to drink — and after the stale recycled water we had been drinking for so long, how fresh and clean and cool the lake water tasted! Everyone laughed again, and passed the cups from hand to hand, exclaiming.

The Guide said they must set a guard over the camp all night.

"Any kind of living thing, harmless or savage, may

be here," he said. The wilderness seemed so beautiful and so still it was hard to believe that, but they chose five of the men to take turns on watch.

And only just in time, for soon after the watch was chosen, the night came upon us. A curtain of deep lilac light swept across the lake, obscuring the sight of the mountain, and sinking almost at once to a deepening purple, then inky darkness. It got dark much quicker than it would have done on Earth — in less than half an hour. The darkness was complete for a moment or two; and then as our eyes got used to it, it was pierced by hundreds of bright and unknown stars — nameless constellations shining overhead. People began to spread their bedding in the tents, and to settle to sleep, and as they did so, a gust of air shook the tent walls, and there was a sighing sound of wind in the woods, and a lapping of water on the shore close by, unseen in the dark. And then the air was quite still again, and it began to rain, heavily and steadily, though the stars were still bright and clear above. When Pattie fell asleep, she could hear Father and Malcolm talking together in low voices at the other end of the tent.

"There must be no dust at all in this atmosphere," said Malcolm. "That would scatter light and delay the dark. No wonder it feels so invigorating to breathe."

Father took his turn on watch, but nothing stirred all night, he said. The rain stopped in an hour or so, and not so much as a gust of air moved anywhere around.

At the sudden return of daylight, all was well.

The next day the land hopper was fitted out. It was a small craft that could carry four men and a scanning viewer to make tapes for the computer in the spaceship. It could hover about forty feet up and glide over water and dry land. It was going to explore the whole planet, looking above all for any sign of life, any possible enemy creature. It had a navigation program built in, sensitive to the planet's own gravity. A lot of people wanted to go on the trip, and the Guide had to choose the crew like a raffle, pulling names out of a bag. Father stayed. The people who stayed would have to look for materials to build houses. Tents would not do forever.

Of course, we went first to the woods, to cut down trees. A party of grown-ups went, carrying saws and axes, and the children went with them to watch. The light in the wood was all ruby-red and crimson where the sun struck down through the red leaves overhead. The trees wouldn't be cut down. The saw blades were blunted as soon as they cut through the soft grey bark. The trees were far harder than wood on Earth. Arthur suggested trying a hacksaw, and that did better, bringing out of the cut in the tree trunk a fine silver dust like metal filings. The work went very slowly and was very boring to watch; after they had been working an hour, the cut was only an inch or so deep.

Father began walking around the wood, looking for twigs on the ground. When he found some, he broke them and held the broken ends to the light. He showed Arthur and Joe what he saw.

"Look, this stuff has a different structure from wood. It's made of lots of little rods joined together. It's very hard to saw, but I guess it will be easy to split."

"I hope you're right," said Arthur. "It will take ten years to build a single house if we have to saw planks and it takes as long as this!"

"And how long would it take to plane and shape wood for window frames and furniture?" asked Jason's father.

"Children, go and gather up as many of these twigs as you can carry, and take them down to the beach," Father said. "We don't even know if this wood will burn yet, and if it doesn't burn, we will have to find something else for fuel." So the men took turns at the hacksaw, and the children gathered twigs all morning.

Father was right about the splitting. The tree trunk that had taken so long to cut through across the grain split easily and straight along its length when wedges were banged in at one end with a hammer.

"We could use them just like this," said Arthur. "Round sections outward, flat edges in, like log cabins."

"As for windows," said Father, "I doubt if we'll need them" — for the sunlight was striking through the pale stuff of the split log as though it were frosted glass. A little more trial and error showed that nails were useless. Even the best ones turned their points at once on the tree trunk, but it was very easy to drill, and the screws they had brought would hold well in it.

Meanwhile, on the beach, Joe set light to the pile of twigs the children had carried from the wood, and discovered at once that the trees would burn. The twigs caught fire easily and blazed brilliantly with a bright blue flame, so hot and fast-burning that the fire had to be dampened with sand before the meal could be cooked on it. "We shall need to be careful making huts out of this," said Malcolm. "We shall need stone chimneys and hearths, I think."

When we had eaten, and brewed a can of coffee on the fierce little bonfire, we quenched it with water, and then the children found in the ashes curious shiny lumps of molten stuff, too hot to hold, and streaked in green and blue and orange, which had formed on the sand where the fire had blazed. A conference was going on among the grown-ups. Cutting trees was going to be a terrible labour, and would soon blunt all the blades we had. They had tried axes instead of saws, but though the axes would split the tree easily, they just bounced off the side of the trunks.

Father looked thoughtfully at the fused lumps in the dead fire. "What if we tried fire?" he asked. "Perhaps heat would soften the stuff."

"We'd have to be very careful," said Malcolm. "It does burn very easily, and we don't want to start a forest fire."

So when they had eaten, the work party returned to the forest edge, and looked for a tree standing apart from its neighbours. A can of fuel was fetched from the supplies, and poured slowly and carefully in a ring around the foot of the tree. The grown-ups brought buckets of sand from the lake shore, to muffle the fire if it got out of hand. Then they lit the ring of kindling around the base of the tree. The flames roared up the tree, burning the bark off very fast, to the very top, and running along the branches to their tips. At the bottom, where the trunk was ringed with fire, a soft red glow began to show on the bare translucent trunk. Then, using the longest saw blade they had, so that they could stand back clear of the fire, the men began to saw through the red-hot band of the tree trunk — and the wood cut like butter, smoothly and easily. The tree toppled and fell, crashing through the outermost branches of neighbouring trees, and thudding on the ground in a shower of torn twigs and leaves. Everyone cheered and shouted.

"Right," said the Guide. "That's how. Now who? Who volunteers to fell the trees for huts? Who volunteers to find isolated trees? We shall need many of them."

Pattie expected Father to volunteer, since he had found how to do it, but he didn't. He went back to Shine with the Guide and began to help plan where the huts would be, and what they would be like. Joe joined the logging party. Pattie and Jason volunteered to find trees. There were a lot of scattered single trees of great size standing among the rocks where the wood petered out at the edge of the lake. Running around

finding them was fun.

The huts were lovely when they were made. They were fluted because the round side of the split trunks faced outwards. They were shiny silver-grey, and the light shone softly through the walls, so they needed no windows at all. The roofs were made of thin slices of wood — it split so easily these were simple to make, and seemed more likely to last than thatch. It made the roofs look like lizard skin, with overlapping scales. Each hut had a tall chimney made of big rough stones fixed with lots of cement. The cement had come on the spaceship, but the sand to mix it had come from the lake shore, and gave it a soft pink tinge. By day a pale grey shadowy light filled the huts, falling through roof and walls, and at night the fires in each hut made bright red flickering patterns over the walls, and you could see the warm glow through the cabin sides from one hut to another. The work went forward steadily, from dawn to dusk, managing a hut each day, by working in gangs — one splitting trees, another building chimneys, another putting up walls and roof. They made one hut for each family, and a big hut in the middle of the site for a meeting-house. Each hut had a vegetable plot beside it, and behind Shine, on the wide plain that lay between the lake and the spacecraft's landing place, they began to mark out fields.

They made a chicken run, and a rabbit run, putting the hutches from the spaceship at one end, and wire netting on poles to make the enclosures. Every day, the chickens were to be fed on corn and millet from a big supply sack; but the rabbits were given not quite enough of their food, to encourage them to eat the strange grass on the new ground.

Chapter Three

With so much going on, it was only the children, only the smallest colonists, who could run around and play, and wander while everyone else was working. So it was Pattie and Jason who found Boulder Valley.

It was by getting lost that they found it. They had walked together along the lake shore, finding little pink transparent pebbles at the water's edge, and watching jellyfish. The lake had swarms of jellyfish in it, very bright green jellyfish, which bobbed around, and oozed themselves into funny shapes to wriggle along. Pattie and Jason walked a long way on the beach, and when they got tired, swam in the lake. Then they began to walk back to Shine, and it seemed they had been on the way back for some time and they still couldn't see the village huts.

"Let's take a short cut," said Jason. "If we go over that hump of land there, it should get us home a shorter way."

Pattie followed him. But when they climbed the hump of land that jutted out from the hills toward the lake, and looked over, they found they were not looking down at Shine but down into a strange new valley.

It was a scooped-out shape, gently sloping and curved. They ran down the slope into the valley. It was like standing in the bottom of a bowl, or nearly like that, except that one edge of the bowl was missing, and through the break in the rim of hill the lake could be seen. There were a few scrubby bushes with bright crystalline blue flowers on them, and a lot of brown boulders scattered around all over the lower slopes and the valley floor.

When Pattie and Jason called to each other, their voices seemed very loud and clear, as though the hillside was talking back at them in their own voices.

When they crossed the bowl of the new valley and climbed up to the top of its far side, they found themselves where they had expected to be before, on one of the ridges that bounded the plain of Shine, and in sight of home.

Pattie took Father and Sarah and Joe to see the valley a few days later, when the Guide ruled a rest day.

"A natural amphitheatre," Father said. "Perhaps we should have made our village here."

"Oh no, Father," said Sarah. "Think of having to shift all these rocks!"

"I like the rocks," said Pattie. "They're fun to climb up and jump off!" And she showed them, by climbing up the nearest one.

"It's odd," said Joe. "I wonder why they're all rounded like that?"

"Glacial boulders?" wondered Father. "But why all here, and none on the plain?"

"Well, thank goodness for that," said Joe. "Sarah's right. It would be terrible work if we had to clear them to plough."

Sarah was sitting on one now, chanting to herself, and listening to the sound of her voice ringing around the bowl of hillside.

"I'm the King of the Castle, get down, you dirty rascal . . ."

"Can't you think of anything better to say than that?" demanded Father. And he began to say, very loud and clear,

> "I wandered lonely as a cloud,
> That floats on high o'er vales and hills,
> When all at once I saw a crowd,
> A host of golden daffodils."

Then he stopped and shook his head. "I can't remember any more."

Then Pattie said, "What's a cloud, Father? What's a daffodil?" and then wished she hadn't, because it made Father look suddenly sad.

"Don't you even remember clouds, Pattie?" he asked, and took her hand in his for the walk home.

When she could get Sarah by herself, Pattie asked about clouds. Sarah said they were big white bolsters in the sky which made it rain. But on the new planet there weren't any things in the sky, and every night as darkness fell, a downfall of rain came close after it, very heavy and sudden, so that you fell asleep with the sound of it on the roof; and by the middle of the night it had stopped, and the mornings dawned bright and clear, with beads of moisture on every branch and leaf.

"You can't *have* rain without clouds," Sarah said. "What comes here must be a kind of dew. Dewfall. I like it better. Rain used to spoil the days at home."

The day after the trip with Father to see Boulder Valley, the land hopper finished orbiting and came back. The explorers were very impressed with the village. And they had found out a lot. They went up to the spacecraft right away, to put the tapes they had made during their flight through the computer. The computer would be able to manage just this last task, then the battery cells would be used up and there would be no more super science from the Earth to help them.

When the tapes were processed, all the people met in the big hut that had been made for gatherings. The Guide told us the news.

"We are on quite a small planet," he told us all. "More like the moon than the Earth. We are orbiting a bright sun, but we are orbiting much more evenly than the Earth; there will be less difference between one season and another here. Such small difference as there is suggests that it is spring now, and time to plant. As you all know, there is seed enough for one sowing, and a small reserve. The soil here seems fertile, though, as you also all know, the plant life here is crystalline and might act on our digestive systems like ground glass, so we can only eat what we can grow from Earth seeds. It seems there is no life in the waters of this planet except algae and suchlike, and the jellyfish we have all seen. Tomorrow, therefore, we must catch some and see if they can be cooked and eaten, unpalatable though they look."

Cries of "Ugh!" from the children were scolded quiet when he said this.

"As for land life, of a kind which might compete with us, or threaten us, or give us animals for farming, the tapes show no signs of any such life over the greater part of the land surface. However, Peter, our expert, will tell you about this."

Peter was a tall, bearded man. The children knew him because his choice of luxury had been the funny little chess set that let you play the game with another person instead of with the computer, and he had played with them sometimes on the journey.

"There's just a slight oddity in the record," said Peter. "Signs of biorhythms, very slow ones, somewhere on the lake shore, near here. I'm baffled. There are two possibilities. One is that the computer is not operating perfectly. It is supposed to discount biorhythms which we produce ourselves, and so tell us about any *other* form of life; perhaps it isn't screening us out perfectly. The other possibility is that something here produces an effect *like* a biorhythm — though, as I say, an extraordinarily slow one. The effect is only hereabouts, and it's a bit of a coincidence if it's nothing to do with our presence here. And nobody has seen anything except the jellyfish, so I think we can safely assume that there is in fact no animal life on this planet. We have the land to ourselves."

The grown-ups were still talking in the meeting-house, making plans for ploughing and sowing, stockpiling timber, and sharing out food rations to last till harvest, when Pattie fell asleep in her chair, dreaming of eating jellyfish and being sick. Sarah picked her up and carried her across in the open under the stars, to put her in her bunk in their own hut.

Pattie didn't eat jellyfish, and wasn't sick the next day, and neither was anyone else. For as soon as the horrible gluey mass of the fish was heated up, smelling funny, within moments of it beginning to boil in the pan it broke into flames and began to burn. It burned with a tall bright green flame like a firework, except that it gave a clear, steady, greenish light. Malcolm became excited and began to try to work out ways of using jellyfish as fuel; he said they must be full of oil of some kind. Jason's mother, however, just took a ladle and took a scoop of the burning pan in a bowl to make a lamp in her house, and that idea seemed very easy to use. Jason's mother wanted light to sew by, sitting at her fireside after nightfall, but of course nearly everyone had something they would like to do in the evening, and so Shine was transformed. For the buildings at night were now a soft pale green, with points of emerald visible where the lamps were hung, and the leaping glow of the fires made a ruby-red glow in the middle. The blurred and magnified shadows of the people moving inside their houses cast dark figures softly over the walls of the fluted, shimmering green and red shining houses, and Shine at night looked like a scatter of blocks of fire opal, lying on a dark land under the stars.

So life at Shine began to settle down. After the exploration party returned, there were no more night watchmen, and everyone slept in their bunks at night. The grown-ups needed their sleep, for now the work of ploughing began. There was fuel enough in the land truck to draw the plough this time. In later years, it would have to be pulled by teams of men, but we hoped that in later years the ground would be easier to turn than it was this first time.

The grey glass grass broke and crumbled and disappeared into the black earth under the ploughshare. Peter and Malcolm tried to sow the wheat by scattering it in handfuls, as Father said had once been done on Earth, before anything useful had been invented. But they soon stopped, because it was lying in clumps, and some was getting lost over the edge of the ploughed ground, and it was so precious we wanted every single grain to grow. So we began to plant it, dropping it seed by seed. The children were better at this job than grown-ups, because they had such small fingers and thumbs to take the seeds between, but it was terribly slow going. And Father didn't come to help. For three days he just wasn't there when the work was being done, and people began to notice and make remarks about him, and Jason's mother even asked the Guide what the rules were about people not working, and the Guide said the rules had run out, as the fuel was doing, and we had to get along without any.

Father was making a seed drill. He got the idea out of his book on technology, and he made it out of wood. It was a box on wheels — Father got some wheels from a trolley from the spaceship, and put them on his box. It had a row of holes in it which dribbled a little trail of wheat grains neatly into five furrows at a time. When the drill began to work, everyone stopped grumbling about Father, and congratulated him.

At supper that night, he began to talk to Joe and Sarah, and Pattie too, though perhaps he thought she was too young to understand him.

"I plan to be the contriver, the maker for this planet," Father said. "The plan brought Peter and Malcolm to be experts, and Arthur who knows about farming, and so on ... You know how the plan goes. But when that spacecraft runs down, it is only metal junk, useful metal junk. Peter won't have any computers to be expert about. We want a different kind of expert — the kind who long ago helped the poor people on Earth. They needed, not machines exactly, but *gadgets* — things you can make out of wood and string, things you can make and mend yourself, like the seed drill. The book I brought is full of ideas like that one. I will be a maker. When the harvest is in, I'm going to make a loom, and a spinning jenny, and find something we can spin and weave."

"We aren't short of clothes and cloth, Father," said Sarah. "And I think there are three sewing machines. Funny ones — you have to turn them by hand."

"We will be short, Sarah," Father said. "How long do clothes last? How often did you need new jeans and T-shirts at home?"

"And you mean we won't farm, we'll make and sell stuff?" she said. "Is that fair?"

"Why, no, my dear," he said. "We'll do our share of the work. And we'll share what we make, as long as the others share with us. But we will be important. We will be very respectable citizens here. We will hold our heads high. You don't realize, I think, how divided and snobbish the old world was. Nobody counted for anything without a degree in maths and computing, and ecological science, and I was just a plain mechanic. Did you wonder why we were chosen for the escape? I'm just population fodder — no wife, and three healthy children with good genetic make-up, that's why. We are just muscle power in the plan, just labourers. But I think different. I think, in a world without machines, science won't be so useful; make do and mend will count for more. Humble gadgets;

practical things ... I'm good at those. Those will be my contribution, and your contribution, and we will be as good as anyone here, I promise you!"

"Oh, Father," said Joe. "You're wrong. Everyone on this expedition counts for something. We are all in it together, and all equal. You don't need to fuss."

"Well, well," said Father. "We'll see."

Chapter Four

When the wheat was in the ground, a bad time began. At first the grown-ups were pleased with themselves. Everybody had worked hard. The harrow from the spaceship had been hauled over the furrows to cover the seeds over. The land truck had pulled it across about half the acres and then run dry. So the men had pushed it out of the way, and begun to drag the harrow themselves, in teams of six at a time. When it was all done, everyone was tired but triumphant. And then we had all to wait and see if it would grow, and if it would not, we would starve.

The first really bad thing that went wrong was all our rabbits dying. We had made them so hungry they had begun to eat the grey grass. One morning when we woke up they were all sick, lying in a heap in a corner of their hutch, with sad cloudy eyes. And by the next day they were all dead. Sarah said they died of homesickness; Father thought they might have caught some kind of virus; most people thought they had been killed by eating the crystalline plants. The chickens were all right; and they had eaten only Earth-grown grain. All the children were sad about the rabbits; Jason even cried. But it was lucky about the chickens, because we hoped to get some eggs to eat soon. The iron rations from Earth wouldn't last forever.

And, of course, once the sowing was done, there was time to think, and worry. Most families dug their vegetable patches, and planted lettuces and carrots and beans from the seed reserves. And what made the worry worse was that nothing would grow in the vegetable patches. Lettuces didn't come up at all, and carrots came black and hard as bones, and all twisted, so everyone pinned their hopes on the beans. Beans are important food. They grew nice green leaves, though after a while the leaves had mottled patches of glassy clear specks. The pods were a brownish colour when they formed, and the beans themselves just didn't grow inside the pods — they were little withered specks instead of nice fat eatable seeds.

Of course, it took time to find out that the vegetables wouldn't grow; life was full of time, full of waiting. Father kept busy with his gadgets, and Malcolm with testing things to see what we could eat. He didn't find anything much. There was a kind of shellfish, and one or two bitter herbs, but nothing easy and nice. Every time a seed went wrong in a vegetable patch, people got gloomier. Everyone was worried, and everyone except Malcolm and Father was bored. Once you got used to it, life at Shine was deadly. No records, no television, no books, nothing. Once it was dark, you just sat by your fire, lit up bright green by a jellyfish, and gloomed.

Joe read nothing but Father's technology book. Even Sarah didn't want her pony book any more. Ponies were about as relevant on Shine as the natural history of little green men would have been on Earth. That left *Robinson Crusoe*. The trouble was, it all seemed rather silly. He seemed to have it easy compared to us; there was plenty to eat on his island, and when he planted things they grew, and all the time a ship might just come by and take him home, and he seemed such a stiff old bore about it all. We began to read it aloud to each other in the evenings, but we soon stopped. Yet we needed something.

For one thing, just sitting all evening like a zombie soon gets a bit much, and for another, all the things that were happening to us were just slopping around in our heads, and we needed some stories to cheer us up. Stories are tidy; they don't just slop around like happenings. Just once, Sarah said to Pattie, "Oh, Pattie, if only you ..." Then she stopped herself. And it was Sarah who thought of trying to swap our two books for something someone else had brought.

Straightaway she found that three other families had brought copies of *Robinson Crusoe.* And nobody at all wanted her pony story. Various people would have swapped something for Father's technology book, only he wouldn't lend it.

"That doesn't go out of my sight," he said. "Anyone may come and read it here, but here it stays. It has to be kept safe." Sarah made a list of books that were in the colony somewhere, to help her bargain. It was, Father said, "A right job lot." He was very struck by Sarah's list.

"Not one Shakespeare," he said. "Among us all, not one."

There was a *Grimm's Fairy Tales*, though, and one of

the men we hardly knew had Homer's *Iliad.* The problem was that the owner of Grimm didn't want to borrow *Crusoe*, they already had that. In the end, Father got it for us. He traded the loan of it for help in fitting out the family's house with benches and cupboards and beds. He had to work very hard for it, too. Sarah thought it wasn't fair, and asked the Guide, but he just said we must rely on good neighbourliness for such things as lending between families. There weren't any rules about that, and weren't going to be. Father worked for the Grimm because he heard Pattie asking Sarah for the story of "Cindriella and the Three Bears," and he realized that we had forgotten the Earth stories, or muddled them up.

And the sad thing was that the *Grimm* was disappointing when we got it. Father said it wasn't the real thing, but rewritten for children. And the book hadn't been taken care of; it had coggled covers from being left out in the dewfall, and some torn pages. But when Father sat down to read it to us, one soft evening as we sat outside our hut after supper, the children gathered from the nearby houses and sat down to listen with us. Father began to read "The Three Feathers," and very soon grown-ups gathered, too, and stood around listening. And as Father read on, a kind of quietness grew, a kind of strong attention, from the listening everyone was doing, as though it made the words louder and stronger if more people were listening to them. After "The Three Feathers," we had "The Fisherman and His Wife." And then the best of all, "The Boy Who Had to Learn Fear," but that one had pages missing, so we were stopped in the middle without knowing how it ended. You should have seen how cross that made everyone! Some of the grown ups tried to remember the story, but none of them could. Malcolm remembered another one about a girl with very long hair and a prince; the Guide remembered one about a huge, skyhigh beanstalk.

We all sat up very late that night, when Pattie crept away at last, they were all trying to remember *Hamlet*. Later she half woke, and heard the dewfall beginning, and the Guide's voice saying to Father at the door, "The truth is, we didn't value that stuff when we had it, when we could just pick up a book any time. And now it's all dying out of mind, and we must do without, as without so many other things."

And Father said, "God help me, I must have read that story once, and yet I can't remember how it ended. But we have learned fear in our own way here, I suppose. God help us if we must do without our wheat harvest."

"You are right, brother," said the Guide. For in the time of fear and waiting for the wheat, the grown-ups had all begun calling each other brother and sister.

The hard times were all in the mind, really. We were getting good eggs. We still had stores from Earth for weeks. We weren't actually hungry, though we were on half-rations. But every time a carrot blackened, or a

bean plant failed in someone's plot, the worry got worse. And without vegetables to grow, there wasn't work enough, so there was time to worry. The wheat looked all right; in fact, it looked lovely, covering the plain around Shine with a marvellous bright tender green. Little blades like swords stood up through the black ground, and put a green pale haze over the ground, and then grew thicker and stronger, and stood like velvet shining in the sun. A silky look was on the green acres. It certainly didn't look like anything that was native to the new planet — it looked like home, oh, it made people ill with homesickness. It made them sad, and tired and unhappy. Not the young children — it got the grown-ups. And the worry deepened when Bill, who was the farming expert along with Arthur, found that he could break a blade of wheat clean across, snapping it like glass between his fingers. And so fear grew with the wheat, a terrible fear that there would be no way to grow food on the new planet. And we could never go anywhere else; there was only a burnt-out spacecraft to remind us of far journeys, and of course, though nobody ever mentioned it, Earth wasn't there any more. If the wheat failed us, there was only a box of pills that would be kinder than hunger.

Probably it was because the wheat was turning to glass that Bill was so bad-tempered and horrible. As one of the farmers, he felt it was up to him. And day by day the wheat looked less right. It should have been milky green, solid, like leaves on Earth, and it was growing brighter and transparent, till the light struck through the stands of blades in the fields, and they shone like emeralds, and sparkled transparent and clear. There was never any wind on Shine, never a ripple across the wheat or a movement of water in the lake, and that at least was lucky, for a wind would have broken every blade of wheat clean across, it was so delicate and brittle as it grew tall.

Bill was the one who had Homer. Father wanted Homer. He said it was the best book on the planet, since so many people had chosen badly, and the *Grimm* was all torn and incomplete. And Bill wouldn't let him borrow it. Father let Bill come to our hut and read the technology book, but Bill wouldn't even let Father read his Homer without paying. And he wouldn't take any pay except food. And Father wouldn't consider paying in food. We all said we'd do without supper and not grumble if we got a good story, but Father said we were on iron rations now, and it would damage our health to have less.

It was Joe who helped. He understood things better, being older. He heard Pattie and Jason and the other little children playing counting out and skipping games down on the lake shore. When Joe came by Mary was skipping in the rope, and Jason and Ben were turning it, and Pattie was chanting:

There aren't any birds,
And there aren't any bees,

To share the sugar on the candy trees.
One, two,
Two, three,
A suck for you, and a suck for me

"What's that, then, sis?" said Joe. "I don't remember that from Earth."

"Well, of course not, silly," and Pattie. "How could you? There aren't any candy trees on Earth, are there?"

"What do you mean?" he asked. "What are candy trees?"

So the children stopped skipping and took him and showed him the candy trees. They were growing in the wood that the logs for building Shine had come from. They didn't look very different from the other trees, but they had little crimson droplets oozing here and there from the bark. If you put out a finger to touch the droplet, your finger stuck, and when you pulled it off and licked, it tasted sweet. Not just sweet, either, but delicious. Jason showed Joe how to roll up the trickles of ooze into a lovely sticky red lump like toffee to pop in your mouth.

Joe was very pleased. He ate quite a lot, and he told us not to tell anyone else for that day, and he took some wrapped in broken leaves to show Father.

That evening Father took all the sugar we had left and gave it to Bill in return for a read of his Homer. Bill gave him a two-hour read for the sugar. Father came back and told us what he had read. But it was very boring. It was all about some gods quarrelling, and then about some heroes quarrelling. They went to Troy, but then they argued outside the walls, and one of them wouldn't help in the battle.

"I suppose I didn't get as far as the good bits," said Father, "though I read as fast as I could. It's a very famous story."

"What do we do about the candy trees?" asked Sarah.

"Oh, we tell the others now," said Father. "It wouldn't be fair to keep it secret longer. I played a bit of a dirty trick on Bill over the sugar, as it is."

Everyone was very pleased. The grown-ups didn't just go looking for oozy patches of the trees, as the children had done; they cut little grooves in the tree bark, and fixed up empty tin cans to catch the flow. They knew how to do this straightaway, for it seemed that there *had* been candy trees on Earth, though not in the part we had come from.

"It's like maple syrup," Malcolm said. "Good stuff, and energy food for us."

Father explained to Pattie that it would keep them from being very hungry till the wheat could be harvested, but it hadn't the sort of goodness they needed to keep alive and well forever.

Malcolm said, "We should learn from this. There was sweet sap around us all this time, and the children found it for us. There may be other things, fruits or nuts, or berries. We should look and keep looking around the seasons."

But the forest held no more surprise picnics, just plenty of the sweet-sapped trees. And it was just as well that we had pans of tree candy all ready, and plenty of them, because of what happened next.

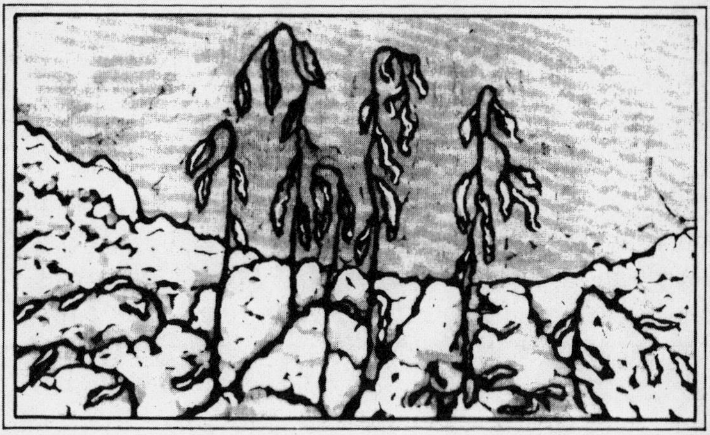

Chapter Five

Again it was the children who found it, or rather found that it was happening. They were all playing in Boulder Valley. Pattie and Jason were in charge of some of the even smaller children — the ones who had been born on the journey — Jason's sister Mary, and Malcolm's smallest, Bob, and some others. All the grown-ups were in a conference of some kind, and Sarah and Joe seemed to count as grown-ups now. The children were in Boulder Valley, playing at climbing up the boulders, and sliding off them again. Pattie had a picnic, the usual iron-rations picnic, in a grey tin from the ship's stores, and she was spreading it out for them on a cloth on the grass. Square grey hard biscuits, and grey-brown chocolate, and pink pasty guava jam.

Pattie liked playing fathers, it made her feel grown-up. She saw Mary some way off and called her back.

"Come and slide on this stone, Mary. We're just ready to eat."

"I'm not sliding on that one," Mary said. "It pushed me off."

"Oh, rubbish, Mary! Come on!"

"It did, it did!" said Mary, coming back all the same when she saw the picnic. "I climbed up it and it shrugged itself and made me fall off."

Jason looked at it with interest, biting a biscuit.

"Its shape looks different from before," he said. So Pattie stared at it too. And while they were all looking, a crack appeared in the stone. It just tore open a little way, and there was an inside like a piece of wet grey velvet.

"I don't like it here!" wailed Mary. "Let's go home!" The stone tore some more. Tore, and moved; not that it moved on the ground, but it moved *inside*, like a person in a sleeping bag shifting arms and legs.

"Let's go *now*!" said Pattie.

They left the picnic just where it was, and began to go, scrambling up the sloping side of Boulder Valley, towards the path to Shine. But, as they went, all the stones in the valley were moving. They were heaving, and shuddering, and tearing open. A very big one lay close to the path home, and as they got near, they saw it had opened right down the middle, and a draggled silver-grey wing, with dark purple blotches on it, lay like a tablecloth across the path.

"We'll be all right," said Pattie very bravely, "if we just run. When I say 'now.' Now!"

And they ran. They ran around the edge of the spread wing, and reached the top of the slope, and stopped for breath, and looked back. All over the bowl of the valley the stones were tearing, and crumpling, and showing soft, furry wings. On the farther side of the valley, one giant moth had got all the way out, and was half fluttering, half crawling on the ground, fanning its wings in the sun. They were losing the damp look and turning a bright dusty silver marked with crimson. Very near them, just below where they stood, the moth whose wing had lain in their way was fighting his body free of the crumpling stone. He was thick grey, and furry, but he had front arms, and a round head like a person, and he was actually *looking* at them, with dark red, vacant, lidless eyes. He made Pattie feel very frightened and very sick, and she screamed as loudly as Jason and took Mary's hand and ran and ran away.

They all ran, screaming and crying into the grown-ups' meeting, and some of the men took guns, and all the people ran back up the hill toward Boulder Valley. But Pattie sat and thought. Now that she wasn't looking at them any more, she wasn't sick at the moth people, even when she remembered she had climbed all over them. She went and asked Jason's mother, who was trying to calm the babies down:

"What do moths eat? Will they eat us?"

"Heavens, no," said Jason's mother. "Moths on Earth ate nectar from flowers, I think. Not *meat*!"

So Pattie went to the cupboard in her hut, and fetched a pan of the lovely tree candy, and started out after the others to Boulder Valley. And as she got to the edge of the village, the moth people began to fly overhead. Their huge beating wings made a wind that stroked Pattie's face and flattened her hair back from her forehead just like wind at home. All those years closed inside the spaceship, and the time on the new planet, had made Pattie forget the air could move, could touch you, as the quiet air of the new place never did. But the eight-foot span of dozens of pairs of wings made the air into wind. Over Pattie's upturned face a great flock of them came, wheeling and turning in the air over Shine, and over the green-turning-gold of the colony's precious wheat field, fluttering down and around, as though they were looking.

One of the huge things alighted just in front of Pattie. It had a round head, halfway between a person's head and a wrinkled walnut; it had trembling antennae, which bent and quivered toward her. It had six legs to stand on, and its body was furry, silver-furry. It folded its wings together above its body, and stood. Pattie closed her eyes, took three steps forward, and put the pan of candy on the ground, and then took three steps back and opened her eyes.

The moth felt forwards towards the candy, and then began to eat it, unrolling a long black tongue and twisting it around the pan. Then it sort of dipped to her, as if bowing, and spread its lovely wings, and flew so close over Pattie's head she ducked. And then she looked up and saw all the grown-ups coming back in a group, and watching her being brave and kind.

After that, we put a big pan of tree candy on the ground outside Shine, as a friendship present to the moth people, and we went and stood, to be scare-crows, scare-moths, around the edges of the field of wheat. For the moth people kept flying, filling the air with the silky sound of wings, and all circling around Shine, as though they were full of curiosity about it. Of course, by and by, some of them fluttered down, as if

they were going to settle on the nodding heads of wheat, and then the Guide fired his gun. Just into the air, just to frighten them. They all fluttered up again, and beat around and around. When that had happened three times, they seemed to understand we didn't want them landing on the wheat, and they kept away. There were a lot of them eating the candy we had given them. Pattie thought it was unkind to fire guns to frighten them, but the Guide told her the wheat was so brittle that anything would break and crush it down, and we couldn't afford to risk it.

"Ah, why bother?" growled Arthur. "We've got eyes. We can all see what is happening to the wheat."

Pattie picked a stem of wheat to look at it close to. Within the folded leaf, the grains were swelling and hardening. She peeled the leaf off, and saw the close-packed grains within. They had edges. She pulled them off the stalk and tumbled them on the palm of her hand. Little shining green glass hexagons, like beads. The wrong shape. Hard and faceted like glass. Pattie looked up from the beads in her hand across the field. It was just turning from pale green-gold to yellow like the crust on bread. It was ripening as it ought to, but it was too shiny, too transparent. Pattie felt frightened. The wheat field was more frightening than the moths.

When it got dark that day, the people of Shine went home to bed, and a watch was set for the first time since the land survey came home. But the moth people didn't sleep, they flew. The soft pulse of their wings beat around Shine all night, and brushed across the glassy walls of the huts. Father said they were drawn by the lights of the fires and the jellyfish lamps. Their shadows fitted across, blanking out the warm glow that showed from neighbouring houses, passing and repassing, blundering into the house walls and making them shake. After a while, people put out the lamps, and damped down the fires, and the moth people were quieter. Malcolm came visiting Father that evening. They talked in the darkness. Malcolm was excited.

"Those very slow biorhythms that showed up on the scanner," he said. "I thought they must have been some kind of mistake, some kind of malfunction in the computer. But I'll bet now they weren't — they were the sleep rhythms of these moths in the chrysalis stage!"

"Do you think they are any danger to us, Malcolm?" asked Father.

"That I can't say," said Malcolm. "Maybe not. They aren't likely to be a competing form of life. They don't seem hostile, do they?"

"Just curious," said Father. "Think — supposing they have consciousness of some kind — they go to sleep in an empty planet, and wake up to find us!"

"What I'd like to know is what they eat at the grub stage," said Malcolm.

"Do they have to have a grub stage?" asked Father.

"Well, who knows?" said Malcolm "Who knows anything here? We must watch them closely, that's all."

The moth people were with us for three days. We tried to talk to them, but it didn't work. The grown-ups tried very hard. They made lots of funny noises through a loud-hailer. They tried sign language. The moth people sometimes flew around, and sometimes settled, and looked at us, but they didn't seem to understand. We might have thought they were stupid if it hadn't been for them joining in the hopscotch. We were all playing hopscotch — the children, that is — down on the lake shore, and a moth person came and made a lot of little flights and landings, alongside us, as though he were jumping, too. So we laughed, and began to play ring-a-roses, and the moth people came and fluttered round us in a ring outside our ring. So then we played Lambeth Walk, all making a long line, and stamping along the beach, and they made a line too, and came with us. We were very happy, and we laughed a lot. Some of the grown-ups came down and watched. Then the moth people began a game of their own, flying in corkscrews, winding around and around each other. We jumped into the air, and twisted as we fell, as though we were trying their game, and we laughed and rolled around on the beach. Sarah ran into the water, and swam, to see if they would share that too, but they didn't seem to like to go near the water. So in the end we were all just dancing. Arthur brought out his squeeze-box, and played creaky music, and children and grown-ups and moth people all danced around, and we were singing "In and out the dusty bluebells ... you shall be my master!" Pattie was even brave enough to go and tap one of the moth people, and sing "Pitter patter pitter patter on your shoulder!" to it. It didn't really have a shoulder, so she dibbled her fingers where its head joined its body, and it swept its wings up and down and up again at her.

At last, when it got dark, we brought out pans of tree candy and gave it to them, and went indoors to our evening meals. Father said it was amazing the moth people didn't talk, and Pattie told him she thought they did — she could just hear them making squeaking noises to each other, very high and faint. Father and Joe decided it was very high frequency sound that only young ears could pick up.

Chapter Six

After a lovely romp that evening, we expected them to come the next morning. But they didn't, and they weren't flying around above us as they had been every day since they hatched out. So in the afternoon we went to look for them. They were all gathered in Boulder Valley — Boulder Valley all smooth and stoneless now. They were settled on the round slopes of the valley, row upon row of them, all round the curving valley sides, wings folded above their heads, and all facing the circular flat valley floor, looking toward the view of the lake and the distant mountain. And on the valley floor a small group of them were slowly moving, and opening and closing their wings.

Anybody would have known how special it was. It felt very hushed, and intense, and though we could not hear the performers, we could tell that the rest of the moths were *listening* — listening in that way that made words huge and grand, as the people of Shine had listened to Father reading from the Grimm storybook. The whole lot of us gathered now, standing on the valley rim, outside the assembly of moth people, watching and staring, drawn into the circle by the feeling, but shut out hopelessly from understanding. There seemed to be a play going on — speeches, and then slow solemn dances, little bursts of flight, little ringing movements, and amazing, spectacular movements of dozens of wings.

"A drama," said the Guide, bemused.

"A mystery play," said Father. And we settled to

watch, sitting on the rough hillside, and staring.

It seemed to Pattie that it all went on a very long time. She didn't want to leave, go home, play instead. But it made her feel terribly lonely, not to understand at all. At last, when the afternoon was halfway over, the players, the dancers on the stage, suddenly rose in flight, in a great spiralling column of wings that mounted and mounted, blazing red and silver in the sun, and the moth audience began to join in, rushing forward down the hillside onto the stage, and then mounting in flight with the others, so that the column of wheeling wings soared higher and higher and seemed to reach a vanishing point in the bright sky. Like a great kite with a long, long tail, flying upward. And when the leaders had finally flown high enough to draw the very last followers off the ground, the column levelled out, and flew away across the lake, toward the mountain.

Behind them in Boulder Valley they left silence. For though their drama had been soundless, and the great rapt fluttering crowd of them had made no noise, the living hush of their play and the dead silence of the empty valley were quite different.

Somewhere over the lake, the cloud of moths broke line and flew onward in a random scattering. Malcolm, watching them through the only pair of field glasses, said, "They're in pairs now. That must have been a mating dance!"

We all stood for a little while, feeling lost and

disappointed, just as it had felt when suddenly there were missing pages in the Grimm story. And we all went home and ate a lot, though it wasn't really hunger that was making us feel empty.

The moth people were gone all the rest of that day, and all night. We missed their dark forms flitting between the huts, casting scudding shadows across the fireshine and lampshine between neighbours. And the next day, too, they were gone. The grown-ups found themselves things to do, but everyone was restless, and the children suddenly found their games boring with no moth friends to join in.

And then towards evening they began to come back. Or some of them did. Fewer than half. They came straggling, flying low over the still water, and as though they were sick or exhausted, or heavily laden. We could see that they were struggling, that their bodies were swollen and heavy, and some of them could not keep aloft, but touched the water, first just with wing tips, and then, as they struggled and failed to fly higher, with wet wings they stuck to the lake surface, and drifted trapped and helpless.

We could only help some, only those that fell into the water just near the edge; the grown-ups waded in and pulled them onto the shore. But many of them died, floating and sinking far out. Those we had saved dragged themselves, crawling, along the land towards Boulder Valley. The lucky ones who were still airborne flew there. Not more than a quarter of them made it,

Peter reckoned. Pattie and Jason hoped more would come home the next day. We left the survivors resting in the rapid dusk.

But the next morning when we went back, carrying tree candy, they were all dying. They had shed their wings, which lay stretched like coloured cloths across the valley slopes; and they had laid eggs — lots of brown boulders, scattered like rocks on the hillsides. They would not eat our candy but lay curled up and quiet, looking very shrunken and ugly and small without their wings. Pattie cried for them bitterly.

"How long will it before more of them hatch out?" she asked Father when he tried to comfort her.

"I don't know, Pattie," he said. "How can we tell? As Peter said, we don't know anything here. But I think it will be a long time, a very long time."

'Why, Father?" asked Sarah.

"Because the bodies, and the shed wings from the last generation of them, had rotted away to nothing when we got here, and only the boulders were left. And I'm almost sure the boulders were much bigger before they hatched than the new ones are. I think they must have quite a lot of growing to do while they are boulders. And I don't suppose boulders grow fast. It might be years before they come again, and I'm afraid we shan't get here to see it."

"You mean, because the wheat has gone wrong?" said Sarah.

"Yes, Sarah, because of that," he said, very sadly.

It still looked lovely, though. While the moth people had taken Pattie's mind right off it, the ripening had burnished the bronzed wheat to gold, and then to a crusty brownness, like baked bread. The day came for cutting it, using a whirring thing with knife blades on it that Father and Malcolm had made. Then everyone had to help, putting gloves on to keep from cutting their hands, and walking along the fallen swaths of wheat, picking it up, and piling it in witches' hats to dry. The first day we were cutting it, Malcolm took an armful of the stalks and laid them on the ground and beat them till the husks fell off the grains. Then he shook the grains in a sieve, to get rid of the chaff, and got a pile of hexagonal yellow beads, shining like golden glass.

People came down from working in the field and looked at it and shook their heads. They went inside their houses, and all the doors were shut, and the silence was like the silence left behind when the moth people flew away. In our hut, Father sat with his head in his hands, and the little blue bottle of last-resort pills in front of him.

But Sarah said, "I'm going to try, I'm going to try, I'm going to try!" She stole a handful of the glass beads, and rubbed them between two stones, and they fell easily into a dry white powder that smelled good. She sent Pattie for a ladle of lake water, and mixed a dough, and rolled it out thin, and made a pancake, and cooked it on the fire. Then, when it looked done, she broke it into four pieces, and gave one to Pattie and one to Joe, and bit into one herself, leaving Father's share in the pan.

Oh, it tasted good! We ate it in three bites. Then Sarah took the last piece to Father.

"No, Sarah, pet," he said. "No. It can't be eaten. It's like ground glass — it will be like poison to us. It will kill us in terrible agony if we eat it . . ."

"We have eaten it, all three, Father," said Sarah.

"It tastes good," Pattie said.

Father went very white. "Oh, my dears," he said. Then he said, "Listen, if it begins to hurt you, I will give you these pills at once. But let's sit together for a bit now." We sat till Pattie fell asleep, leaning over against Father. She half woke when he carried her to bed. Dimly she saw that the Guide was there, and Malcolm, taking away the last quarter of the pan-baked bread, and Jason's mother sitting beside Sarah. Pattie fell fast asleep the moment Father laid her down in her bunk. "Does your tummy hurt, Pattie?" he asked her, but she barely heard him ask, and she was too far asleep to tell him.

And she woke up in the morning feeling fine, and hungry, to the best day on Shine so far. For Sarah was well, and Joe was well, and all the grown-ups were laughing, and teasing poor Malcolm. "Well," he was saying, "it looks granular under the microscope, that's all I can say!"

But every family was rubbing grain between stones,

and making pan bread for breakfast.

"Well, planet," said the Guide, smiling at the mountain. "Get used to us. We are here to stay. And now let's get the harvest home."

Chapter Seven

Everyone was happy. There was lots of work to do. Everyone went up to the field to gather and stack the wheat, the next day, and for days afterwards. Father said we wouldn't need to build a mill, because the grain was so easy to grind, but every family needed a pair of stones for grinding flour, and they had to be found and shaped. We needed a big bunker to store the grain, some to eat, and some for next year's growing. By and by, Father went and fetched some moth wings from Boulder Valley, all faded and limp, and Malcolm brewed up something to steep them in that made them into a kind of stringy soup; and then we dried out the fibres by pouring the soup through a tray of sand and leaving it to dry in the sun, and then the fibres could be spun into thread, using a funny thing like a top on a stick that Father made. He was going to make a loom next. We would all have red and grey mottled clothes out of moth cloth, when our Earth things wore out. We were looking rather ragged already.

When the harvest was in, and we were getting used to our own good bread, we began to see that winter was coming. It got very cold, not just at night and the leaves on the trees turned black and fell off. All the redness in the forest darkened and the grey grass lost its shine.

The grown-ups decided we would need to share all the food, depending on how many there were to feed in each family.

"We have enough," the Guide said. "Enough for us all to live, to live quite well."

"Enough food, yes," said Father, "But the plan didn't give us all we need."

"You must stop hankering after books, brother," the Guide told him. "All that has gone beyond recovery."

"We had better record the shares we are giving out," said Peter. "We can get paper from the spaceship. There must be some computer printout lying around there that we could write on."

But nobody wanted to go and look for it. It seemed as though we didn't want to remember we had come like refugees from so far away; we wanted to feel that Shine was our home, where we would be, and had always been.

Father thought of something. "What about that empty book of Pattie's?" he said. "We could use that."

"No, Father," said Pattie. "Please don't. Please, it's mine!"

"An empty book, Pattie?" said Father. "No use to anyone. And needed for something important. We all have to share, you know that. Joe, go and get it."

Pattie hid her face, and slipped away from the centre of the group. Joe brought the book from under her pillow in the hut, and Father opened it.

And it was full. It was full of writing, very large and round and shaky.

"Heavens!" said Father. "What's this?" He read for a few moments. "It's a story," he said. "About here, about us. It has the moth people in it, and the hexagonal wheat!"

"Read it to us," said Jason's mother, and others joined in. "Read it to us!" Lots of people, all the people of Shine, gathered around Father with the open book in his hand, all eager, and ready to make the words huge with listening to them.

Father turned back and back in the green book to the very first page, and began to read:

"*Father said, 'We can take very little with us' . . .*"

About this Author

Jill Paton Walsh began writing for children to escape 'the boredom of being trapped in a small house alone with a baby that could not yet talk'. Her first book, *Hengest's Tale*, was published in 1966. Since then, she has written over 15 children's books, including *The Emperor's Winding Sheet*, *Goldengrove*, *Babylon* and *A Parcel of Patterns.* She has won several awards and is recognised as one of the leading British children's writers.